3 a.m. Blues

DEDICATION

To Calliope and Erato, without whose constant inspiration I would be nothing

CONTENTS

Acknowledgments i

Denial & Bitterness 3

Coagulated 9

Untitled 5 10

Against My Better Judgment 11

Tainted Love 13

Wallow 15

The Martyr 18

Trigger Point 21

I'm Nowhere 24

More 26

I Used to Want to Sail the World 28

Euphoria: population-unknown 32

Acceptance & Forgiveness 34

Face It 42

Dust 43

Baptism 44

His Side 46

The Circle of Life 47

Muse Talk 48

Take That Step 49

On Writing Poetry 51

New Beginnings 53

Untitled 6 56

Like a Melody in My Head 60

The Girl from Hendersonville 61

Author Biography 64

ACKNOWLEDGMENTS

MANY THANK TO THE EDITORS OF THE MIDWEST WRITER'S GUILD FOR INCLUDING THE FOLLOWING POEMS IN THEIR 2019 ANTHOLOGY: ON WRITING POETRY, I USED TO WANT TO SAIL THE WORLD

3 a.m. Blues

Denial & Bitterness

My body carries the bruises of our love

I've watched you leave so many times I almost expected it.

I was mired and tangled up in your misery and suffering for so long I thought it was my own.

I'll throw my body on the coals of your love if that's what it takes to be with you.

Coagulated

It's surprising the things you find
out about yourself at 3 o'clock
in the morning,
lying on the living room floor
head spinning with drink,
mind racing with regret,
wanting so desperately to send
that message, yet knowing it's
inviting the devil back in,
granting the succubus access
to my vital organs once more,
like the drag of the needle
tracing silhouettes of angels
wings down my arm, veins
clouding with the junk of us.

Untitled 5

Unanswered questions linger in my mind
like lonely souls at last call.

Unanswerable questions hang in the corners
of my mind like cobwebs in the hallway
closet.

Against My Better Judgment

I am scared of you.
I am frightened to the point
of death when you are near.

I am afraid of who I will become.

I don't trust the decisions I make
when you're near.

My emotions are suspect at best.

When we are together
my body betrays me,
my mind contradicts me,
and my heart drives me

against my better judgement

into your embrace.

Tainted Love

I cannot effectively convey the utter
contempt I have for you.

The resentment I harbor in the deepest
recesses of my soul.

Oceans and rivers
lakes and seas
overflow with my hatred,

volcanos erupt and spew
white hot magma,
tectonic plates recoil,
ecosystems perish
glaciers melt,

all in response to the utter disdain

that has infected me

like an airborne fungus;

it's spores seeking to latch onto any and
every memory we shared, damning it to the
fires of eternal regret.

Wallow

I'm on the outside looking in.
Never belonging, always alone.

I walk the streets in darkness.
The only light shines from the windows of
the establishments from which I have been
shunned.

I am a leper, expelled from the city, forced to
wander outside the gates.

It's all my fault.
Dying in a sea of guilt,
doing the backstroke in the ocean of other's
opinions, navigating the

minefield of *could've*
and *should've*

I am destined to fail:
in the court of public opinion
in the eyes of my children
in the eyes of my parents

in the eyes of my Creator?

I have been raised up,
just to be torn down
I have been employed,
just so they can fire me.

I have been loved just so she can say

with no remorse,

that she loathes the very breath

that fills my lungs.

The Martyr

Always watching but never seeing,
always listening but never hearing,
you see precisely what you expect
from me, hearing only that which is
told with whispering voices
in darkened corridors.

I am found guilty before the trial.
The gallows are being built,
the hangman's noose swinging in
the summer breeze,
my sentence being imposed, I am
a *dead man walking*.

Crowds of perfect strangers gather

to see justice served on the deserving.

My face covered with a black shroud,
as to cover any sign of innocence that
may be seen in my eyes.

The noose is tightened around
my wretched neck with the skill of a
seasoned executioner.

The sound of backslaps can be heard
among the crowd.

Handshaking and congratulations doled out
amongst the purveyors of justice.

Last rites (as if I had any) come quick

and rehearsed, like a speech repeated many times.

The sound of the trap door mechanism rings the finality of it all.

Then, white light.

Trigger Point

Seething rage lying just
beneath the surface,
waiting for its opportunity
to show its face to the masses,

scheming and plotting its escape
from the restraints placed on it
by my other self.

Each day I wake,
not knowing which person I will be;
the person I must be, or the person
I want to be.

Do I give in to the primal

nature of the beast?

Tearing and ripping flesh
tissue and muscle,

sucking marrow from bone,
separating the spirit

from the body
from the soul.

Never satisfying
the insatiable hunger,

the instinctual need
to let go,
to stop pretending

stop fighting it, and

evolve into something more.

I'm Nowhere

My mind is everywhere,
but I'm not in any one location.
You couldn't find me if you tried.
Hell, I can't even find myself.

I've been here my whole life, yet
I have no clue as to my whereabouts.

There's a rock, I remember that,
and there's a tree that looks vaguely
familiar.

That house across the street brings back
some memories of a forgotten time.

I feel I will die here, alone, if someone doesn't find me soon.

Where are the search parties?
Where is the posse?

I would gladly commit a crime if I thought it would grant a much-needed sense of urgency to my situation.

Must I do everything myself?

More

Are we ever really happy?

That gnawing, clawing,
insatiable, teeth gnashing
feeling that there's more;
more to experience,
more to explore,
to love
to fuck up
to lose.

The feeling you're just scratching
the surface of life.

That there's not enough

hours, minutes, or seconds
in the day to discover,

pursue and accomplish those things that
were strategically placed just
out of our reach
in the deepest recesses of our soul
inexplicably linked to the very fabric
of who we are.

There's always more.
There has to be.

I Used to Want to Sail the World

I used to want to sail the world,
now it hurts to say your name aloud.

We swore we would tell each other
when we fell out of love, that we
wouldn't waste one another's time,
but it came suddenly and
without warning.

I can count on one hand
maybe two, the times I dialed
your number thinking just a whisper
is all I needed.

Just one word
followed by silence,
*69
and the imagined shock of
realization across your face.
That's enough excitement for tonight.

When you walk away from eternity
does that exempt you from heaven
and hell?

I just need to know if it's too late
to hedge my bets.
I hear reincarnation is nice.

I could come back as a raven
or maybe a silkworm,
and weave my failures
into a nice sized duvet.

I used to want to sail the world,
but now I can't be in the same room
as you without losing the ability
to conjugate vowels.

It was always vowels with us,
our arguments always ending in I-O-U.

Not to say the times in-between weren't
the best we ever had, just that the edges
were sharp and the cuts were deep.

I used to want to sail the world,
nowadays I just want to right the ship,
keep it safely tucked into the harbor

and moored to the shore,

far from the uncertainties of what lie

beneath the surface of the deep.

Euphoria: Pop. Unknown

It is a very regretful and sorrowful day in the city of Euphoria.

Disdain fills the air like a lake-effect weather pattern. Hope had long vacated this place.

Acceptance & Forgiveness

I wish we had been good

for

each other.

I wish we had been better

to

each other.

I guess I just fell in love with the idea of us and wasn't willing to admit that it was over.

That we were over.

You're an amazing person. I've always carried pieces of you with me.

Probably always will.

I don't know what to do with them most of the time.

I take them out occasionally and examine them, hold them tight, then I carefully place them back in my heart.

I've always searched for my identity in other people, circumstances, and things.

I've never stood still long enough to listen to the echoes in the silence.

I've never looked deep enough inside to recognize the many layers and intricate patterns adorning the walls.

Stare long enough into the eyes of

someone you love, you'll lose all sense of self.

Does that mean if I stare into my own eyes, I'll find myself?

Face It

Let's face it,
he'll never be me
and she will
never be you.

Dust

We humans are as complex
of creatures that could've ever been
created; out of dust anyways.

Baptism

It rains on the just and the unjust

the guilty and the innocent

the rich and the poor

the young and the old

the liars and the cheaters

the killers and the saviors

the hardened

the broken

the chosen,

the free and the imprisoned (by whatever

means)

It rains on the fathers and

the mothers

the child, broken home or not.

All of us feel the rain as it falls
from the heavens, washing away
the filth and the mistakes,
along with the hopes and dreams
of mankind.

His Side

"It's not that I don't agree with your prognosis, I just think maybe you're missing the bigger picture here."
He said.
"And besides, you're not getting any younger yourself."

"Hmmmm..."She said, chewing on the end of her pen and jotting down notes in her notepad.

The Circle of Life

To live and die
and be resurrected
from the grave,
only to die of a broken heart,
or a broken hymen
is the only way to go.

Muse Talk

Inspiration strikes me regardless
of my circumstances.

She doesn't care if it is convenient
for me, if I'm in the mood
if my hands are full or tied,
or if I am awake or asleep.

Her only concern is flowing through
my pen and onto the page.

Take That Step

The journey of a lifetime begins with
deciding to take the first step.
Take that first step.
Throw caution to the wind.
The only thing you will end up regretting is
not taking the chance.

Failure doesn't equal regret.

Regret is the symptom of an unfulfilled call
or task that you knew you should take.

Fearing to fail only leads to regret.

There's nothing wrong with failure.

Failure is wholesome.

Failure is pure.

Failure is a wise, wise old man with a
twinkle in his eye.

On Writing Poetry

It's simple, really.
It's all words and phrases.

A word here,
a turn of the phrase there,
a little formatting,

(blood, sweat, self-loathing,
feelings of inadequacy, tears,
gloom, doom, and a few
fingers of bourbon later)

and boom
you have a poem.

New Beginnings

New life springs forth from the
decaying corpse of unrequited love

It's not difficult to find someone to sleep with...

what I want is someone who's worth going to breakfast with...

Untitled 6

It's not about the sex, it's about the
connection.

It's about the mingling of two souls in
jubilant ecstasy.

Sex is just the vehicle that takes you there
and kind of drops you off on the curb, leaving
you wondering where you go from here.

She says more with her eyes than most people do with their entire bodies

Like a Melody in my Head

You know how sometimes you wake up
singing a song that you haven't heard
in forever, yet there it is in your head?

The melody is catchy and the lyrics
are a page pulled right out of your own life?

That's you.

You are the song forever trapped
in my head.

The Girl from Hendersonville

You are

the world that can't be spoken of

inside me.

You are

the moments when no word can be uttered

for fear of lessening them.

You are

the endless memories that we will share.

You are

the symphony I never composed,

the masterpiece I never painted,

the novel left unwritten.

You are

everything that I could possibly conceive of

in a wife, mother, woman, companion.

You are

my very best friend.

You are

the best of everything that is

good in the universe.

And for that, I love you.

Joseph Fulkerson is a writer of poetry and haiku. 3 a.m. Blues is his second collection of poetry. His first collection 'The Glenmore Sessions' was published in 2019. His work has been included in several print and online publications. He currently resides in Owensboro, Kentucky.

Also Available from the Author

The Glenmore Sessions: A Collection of Poetry

www.Josephfulkerson.com

reedsy.com/discovery/book/the-glenmore-sessions-joseph-fulkerson

Made in the USA
Middletown, DE
29 October 2020